A LONG BRIGHT COLD DARK SUMMER

A LONG BRIGHT COLD DARK SUMMER

A Collection of Poetry and Spoken Word

PJ

PHOENIX JAMES

A LONG BRIGHT COLD DARK SUMMER

For any questions about usage, please email contact@PhoenixJamesOfficial.com

First Edition: 2023

ISBN: 978-1-7396788-9-0 (Paperback)
ISBN: 978-1-7394810-0-1   (Ebook)

Cover Photo by Phoenix James
Cover Artwork & Design by Phoenix James
Book Design & Formatting by Phoenix James

Visit the author's website at www.PhoenixJamesOfficial.com or email him at phoenix@PhoenixJamesOfficial.com

DEDICATION

Frank Williams
and all bright young souls
who brought us sunshine
but then suddenly left
letting the cold in
far too soon.

CONTENTS

ART TO LIFE 1

CAKE 3

CLAY 5

CLEARER PERSPECTIVE 7

CREATIVE PROCESS 10

DREAM ANGEL 12

HAPPY WITHOUT A DADDY 14

HAVEN'T VISITED CAMDEN IN A WHILE 17

HEAVEN HEREAFTER 18

HIGH OFF THIS MOMENT 20

HIRE POSITION 23

I COULD BE MARRIED NEXT WEEK 25

IF HARRIET TUBMAN WAS A VLOGGER 29

ILLNESS OF THE CROWD 31

INSTITUTE OF BARBERSHOP PSYCHOLOGY 34

IT'S TEARING ME APART 38

KEEPING HER HUSBAND SATISFIED 42

LEARNING TO WIN 45

LISTEN UP 47

MOMENTS IN TIME 49

NO EXTRACURRICULAR ACTIVITIES 51

ONE LIFE 53

ONE STONE A DAY 55

ONE TYPE OF MOVIE I REALLY ENJOY 58

SHE SOUNDS TOO GOOD TO BE TRUE 62

SHE'D HAVE TEN HUNDRED ORGASMS 64

SOMETIMES SEX DISGUSTS ME 66

STYLISH DESIGNER COAT 68

TATTOO EXPRESSION 70

THE IMPORTANCE OF FOREPLAY & ORAL SEX 74

THE NECESSITY OF LETTING THINGS OUT 81

THE NEXT BEST THING 83

THE RIGHT WAY 85

THE SECRET WAR 87

THE WORKINGS 90

TRACES OF YOU 92

WE HAVE KIDS, PLEASE DON'T SHOOT 94

WHAT I KNOW 97

WHAT YOU DON'T KNOW WILL THRILL YOU 99

WHEN I'M GONE 102

WHO SHOULD PAY ON A DATE? 106

WHY I MIGHT NEVER GET MARRIED 109

YOU'RE ON YOUR OWN 114

YOUR AUTHOR 119

ART TO LIFE

I love the active involvement of creating
I love the process
The many various processes
That one can go through
In making a piece of art
Any piece of art
I like the inner workings
Of what brings a piece of art to life
Be it music
Be it a poem
Be it a dance
A song
Whatever
I just love the process
You have to love the process
Because as an artist
As a creative person
You spend most of your time
In the process
Of the making of the thing
The thing is what people see at the end
The end point of where the artist
The creator
Abandons the piece of art
Because they say
The work is never done
The artist just abandons it basically
Or calls it an end
When they could actually go on

And sculpt the ear a little bit more
Shape the chest a little bit more
Or whatever it is they're making
Or add another brush stroke
Or a little bit darker here
Or raise the saturation there
In a film
Or you could go on forever
Playing
Fiddling
And tweaking a piece of art
Making it great
And as perfect as possible
But it's never really finished
The artist just decides
It's good enough.

CAKE

What an amazing feat
I have never seen a cake do that
Usually a cake is just supposed to be eaten
You know, prepared and presented
Desired and just devoured
Never would I have imagined this
For such a cake
A cake like this is not supposed to fly
I mean, this was no ordinary basic cake
She slowly picked it up from the table
A cake bigger than the size of her head
And wider than the width of her shoulders
She threw it like an olympic athlete
With such force
With such anger
Way across the room it went
Cakes like that aren't made to fly
But this one did
Her husband
And the woman he was talking with
Now both wearing cake
Collected themselves and left together
Which under any other circumstance
Might have seemed odd
Other guests wiped cake from themselves
As best they could
The music had stopped
And it was safe to assume
The party was over

As we all gathered our things
And filtered out the door
She sat sobbing in the mess
I've never seen a cake like that
After today
It's fair to say
I'm not the only one
Who would be happy
To never see another cake like it again.

CLAY

Kissing your nipples
Breasts
Licking your lips
Listening to your breaths
As hot sweat
Drips
From my forehead
And onto your neck
Glistening
Wet
Warm
Sticky
Sex
Slipping
Legs
Gripping
Skin
Your navel
Pool of sin
Our bodies
Swim
Our soul
Pulls me in
Within
Our minds
Twins
My eyes
Seeing god
In a human being
Where have you been
You say here

Searching for me
In every dream
Naked
Masturbating
Until you fell asleep
Waking
To find
None of them were me
Or yours to keep
You reach
For my hand
And squeeze
So tight
Like death
Holding on to life
Like giving birth
To a new you
You spasm
And you orgasm
In the heights
Of our passion
Like it's a new fashion
We wear each other out
And then calmly lay
Cooling and clammy
Like damp clay
We smile like children
And I say
You were fashioned for me
In every way.

CLEARER PERSPECTIVE

I've walked across to the car park
Just sitting watching the sunlight
I'll watch it for a while
While it's out
Get the sun on my face for a bit
I went touring with the film stuff
Back now
I went to Chile
I went to Mexico
Went to Japan
I went to Ecuador
I went to Germany four times
I went to France
Luxembourg
America
I went to a good few places
A whole lot of traveling
To all those countries
And back now
Back now with clearer perspective
On what I'm doing
What direction I want to go with life
And everything involved
It's a good time
It's a good place I'm in right now
More direction
More focus
It was all up in the air before
Not really having a focus

But is it ever focused
We make plans and God laughs
Who knows
It feels more directed
It feels like there's more direction
To stuff I'm doing
And where I'm going
At least in my own mind
I don't know how it looks on the outside
But to me it feels focused
And it feels I have a lot more clarity
That's the word for me
Clarity
It's a more clear perspective for me
And things I want to do
And where I want to go with things
I didn't have that before
And that's what makes now so good
You just feel more like
You know what's going on
That may change
That can change in a year
Or two or three
But in the moment
We're always in a now moment
I think in the now moment
It's nice to feel like you know
Where you're fucking going
That's just how life is
It's nice to be in that moment
Of, Oh fuck yeah

I'm figuring this shit out now
Yeah, this looks right
That's kind of where I'm at now
And so I feel good
I feel good in that space
In two years, I could say
Fuck this shit
What was I thinking
But right now
It feels it feels positive
It feels in the right direction
And that's good for me
I can work with that
I can work with that level of clarity.

CREATIVE PROCESS

I love the making
And the inner workings
I always want to know
How the artist works
It may be so far away
From what I create
What that artist is making
But I just adore people's creative process
Because I understand what that is
I understand where they have to go
In order to make themselves be able
To create that thing
Or produce that thing
I'm just so for that
Not everybody is
But I love that
And you have to I think
In all great art and creativity
You have to love going to that place
And disappearing outside of yourself
Or inside of yourself
In order to bring that work to life
To not be subjective
And to be subjective
Where necessary
To dance in between the two
And it's all very inner body work
And out of body work
It's a very involved process

But uninvolved at the same time
You have to separate yourself
From the work you're doing
Whilst also being in it
As the creator
It's a very interesting place to be
When in that creative process
And I know my own
Is always new to me
Because it's always a new thing
But I'm even doubly fascinated
When it's someone else's
Where I'm not even in that field
Of creativity
I just enjoy watching art come together
And hearing from an artist
How they reach their process
And what their process is.

DREAM ANGEL

Your heat to my heat
Like flame to flame
Your body against my body
Warm hands and warm exchange
You touch me so softly
And cautiously
Like you're afraid
Like it's all you've ever dreamed of
You say you feel closer
Than anyone has ever let you go
And I say nothing
Because I know
I can feel your anticipation rising
Just like mine
And I'm just... high
Your love is a vibe
All I want us to do right here
Is take our time
Like clouds
The hours quietly float by
And we
Like two angels
Suspended
Embracing in the sky
Existing on air
Entangled in each others wings
Exiting all that is now
Marrying ourselves away
To a heaven elsewhere

You came prepared to love me
And I have waited
For as long as a man can wait
My soul
My company
My truth
My serenity
And not a day too late
I am ready to ascend with you
Unto that sacred place
You draw me out with such care
As gently as you draw me in
To your aura
To your eyes
To your lips
To your skin
If this is all a dream
Please don't ever wake me
Leave me right here
Content in this illusion
And let this stunning angel take me
As we both lay here out of place
Mesmerised in space
My eyes memorising your face
To take back down to earth with me
To dream of you
Just in case.

HAPPY WITHOUT A DADDY

I think there were moments growing up
Where I felt I wish I had a dad in my life
I wish I grew up with my dad
I was my dad was around
I wish I did those things
A person does with their dad
But it's not there
So you don't know what it's like
Or as much as you think you might enjoy it
Or you you're missing out on something
You're still not experiencing it
So you still don't know
What it's like to have it
You're just fantasising in a way
I couldn't say now
Whether I feel I missed out
For one, I would've been
A completely different person I think
If I had that father figure
Or my dad in my life growing up
Myself and my mum and my dad
In the same house growing up
The dynamic would have been different
So I would have grown up
As a different child
My outlook
Would have been different on life
So my experience
Would have been different

So essentially
I would've been a different person
I quite like who I am
And how I think
And how I deal with life
How I compute
So I don't know
If I would look at it like a loss
Or I missed out
Maybe I gained, who knows
We'll never know
But now, I feel like I'm in a good place
And I feel like I gained a lot of strength
From being in that situation
Having to do certain things as that child
Who didn't have their father
To go to as a man
Or as a boy growing into a man
Your father would be there to guide you
I didn't have that
I had to do a lot of that on my own
So there were certain strengths
That came from that
I would want to go back
And change that
It would be changing me
I don't think I feel like I missed out
I feel there was an element
Of growing up as a kid
And having your father around
That I didn't experience

But I don't know what type of child
Or adult I would have turned out to be
Having that dynamic
I can't say which way it would have gone
I won't know now
I can only know the side that I'm living
And I'm quite happy with that side.

HAVEN'T VISITED CAMDEN IN A WHILE

Camden Town
I haven't been down there for a while
Maybe around year
I've haven't been up that way
I had a girlfriend up that way
But then she pissed me off
So I don't have a reason
To go up there anymore
I haven't been up there for a while
I used to be down there performing
Or going out to places up there
The Jazz Cafe
Bars, food stands, restaurants
The indoor market place and all that
But I haven't been up there for a while.

HEAVEN HEREAFTER

What if
The idea of a blissful heaven
Beyond this life on earth
Was simply just an imagined place
Created in the mind of man
That allowed him to better cope
With suffering
Perhaps heaven
Doesn't exist at all in reality
Outside of the mind
What if
The notion of an afterlife
Is just a pacifier we give to ourselves
To soothe and comfort us
From the thought that this life
With all of its pain and disease
And discomfort
Is all there is
That there must be some recompense
Somewhere elsewhere
Beyond here
For not being allowed to stay
Or to take all of our loved ones
And worldly possessions with us
When we're forced to pass on
Maybe the existence of heaven
Is just what we've convinced ourselves of
So we don't have to face a reality
That the brevity of this short life

Is all we get
And there's nothing else after
That those gone before us
Are not gone completely
That we will see them each and all again
In an abundant life hereafter
Somewhere out there
What if the haunting finality of a last breath
Is just too much for man to accept
And thus he appeases himself in the belief
That there is more to see
In a life
After death.

HIGH OFF THIS MOMENT

How amazing it would be
If you could go into a place
Or a platform like YouTube now
And you could look up
Your great-great granddad
Or great-great-great-great granddad
Or grandmother
Doing something
Like boiling an egg
Or talking to a friend
About a new pair of shoes they bought
And how they either like them
Or don't like them
Or for what reason they like them
Just having a random conversation
Nothing that would be anything
To anyone else but you
How amazing that would be
How much do you think
That privilege would be worth
If you could go and do that
Just go on the internet
And just see way back
To where you came from
Way down the line
Your great-great-great grandmother
Or great-great-great-great granddad
Just tying his shoelace or something
If we had shoelaces back then

I think that would be so amazing
The thing is
You now are that
That great-great-great-great
Great grandparent
Whether you're a sister
Whether you are a daughter
Whether you are an auntie
You are that person now
You're that person
That someone in the future
Generations and generations
In the future
Will be looking back to see
Seeing where they came from
You're that person now in history
And time
Within this very moment
You're that person
That someone is going to be
Looking back for
Looking at your nose
Looking at your lips
Listening to your voice
Looking at what you wore
Thinking how much they look like you
Or the mannerisms that they have
They can actually see they came from you
How amazing is that
To say, Oh look
That's where my eyebrows came from

It's crazy when you think about it
We're living in that time now
Where people are going to be able
To reference back
And see that stuff
Because the technology is here now
It's here
We're living it
It's amazing
I'm high off of this moment
That we're living in right now.

HIRE POSITION

You've told me a couple of times
When you'd be starting back at work
But I can't remember
When you said it was
It'll be a long time you'll be off
Deep into the summer
You'll still be relaxing
That's awesome
That's one good side of being off
Being able to have that time
You earned it
You've been there a long time
But what I hate
Is when you tell me
About all these new managers
That come and want to take the piss
That's annoying as fuck
You know every nook and cranny
Of the building
The way that the building works
And the day to day operations
Way better than they do
And how to deal with the customers
And everything
The cadence of the place
And they come in
New, fresh and green
And want to treat you
Like you're nothing

Because they have a higher position
In writing, on paper
That's some crazy shit, man
That would annoy me
And not only that
I mean, age is just a thing
But they're younger
When I say green
They've just literally left school
And don't know anything
They've never been there
In that environment before
And they want to come and parade
On your fifteen years of service
And some you're twice their age
Or way older than a lot of them, right
Crazy
You know the runnings
And the procedures
And everything
Better than they do
I'm sure there's points
Where you have to tell them
How it goes
Because they're just still learning
They come in not knowing fully
And then they come and want to style
On their higher position
On you
Not acceptable.

I COULD BE MARRIED NEXT WEEK

I'm just being practical about it
I love the idea of meeting someone
And falling in love
And they're all I think about
And that whole thing
When we watch movies
We think, Ah that's nice
I wish that was me
Getting all teary eyed at the end
Ah they found each other
Ah it worked out
You kind of picture yourself
In that situation
I like that
But I have to be practical
About where I'm at in my life
And what I really want
And the amount of time
That's going to take
I really have to be realistic about that
And also about how much time
The kind of relationship I want
Is going to take
And the kind of person
That I want to be with
Would require that time from me also
For it to work
It has to be
Because I can't want that for myself

And be with someone
Who doesn't want that
That's not going to work
There has to be someone
Who wants that
As deeply as I want it
And for me to find that relationship
And exist in that relationship
I have to be in a place
Where I'm comfortable
To pursue that in the way that I want to
It requires time
Long story short
People talk about how you can do both
People do it
Which is fine
But I just know where I'm at right now
And the amount of mental
And physical energy
I need to invest into that
Which is a lot to do with myself
And I'm just not in a place
Where I want to give that mental time
And physical energy to someone
As much as I would love to
The two just won't coexist
It's just not realistic
And I have to be practical
And realistic about that
I feel there's a time for things
And it's just not that time right now for me

That's my take on it
I don't know everything
I'm still learning like everyone else
People have been in relationships
For twenty years
And are still learning things
About their partner
Still learning things
About how relationships work
So where am I at
I've never been in a relationship
For any length of time compared to that
So I'm learning
I could say all that
And I could be married next week
So I can't really say
I just know
That I have certain things
I'm focused on
And I know what level of focus
They require
To succeed
It just means
Me putting certain things
To the back burner
It doesn't mean
That I won't ever pursue them
It just means
That I'm not putting myself
In the way of them right now
In fact I'm avoiding them

I'm avoiding those things
Because I know they're distractions
And I've got an addictive personality
So I know I have to be careful
With what I attach myself to
I have to be strategic
I can't just say
Okay, I'm going to fall in love
Because it will happen
If I focus on it
So I have to be very careful
Where I put my focus.

IF HARRIET TUBMAN WAS A VLOGGER

I just had the craziest thought
It's probably not that crazy really
But I just thought
Imagine if Harriet Tubman
Was a vlogger
Imagine if she had vlogged
If she had a video camera
And she'd video logged and filmed
Everything that took place
With the Underground Railroad
The freeing of all those slaves
Imagine if she had documented
All the meetings
And conversations she had about it
What she was planning
Or not
How it's going to go down
And then, how all the travelling
And all that stuff went down
The actual freeing of the slaves
And she was just vlogging all of it
Could you just imagine
Being able to watch that now
If you could go onto the internet
And watch the whole thing
How much would that be worth
To an individual
Who was interested in history
Wow

I guess it was one of those things
Where it wouldn't have been
Something that
You would have kept evidence of
Necessarily
But I mean, just the idea
Maybe even like a diary
But maybe that was something
That probably wouldn't have happened
You wouldn't have made the point
Of writing down what you're doing
I mean, you probably just had people
On a need-to-know basis type thing
But just imagine, it was like a whole thing
Where she had a video camera
She had a guy or two following her around
Filming and recording everything
Like a small documentary film crew
While she was doing all this stuff
And she wanted to document this time
This moment in history
Because she knew
Down the line, ahead of time
It was a special moment.

ILLNESS OF THE CROWD

Someone once said
Birds born in a cage
Think flying is an illness
And so far as it applies
To the likes of me and you
I've found this to be true
As the social condition of our time
Is conformity
Choosing to be different
You're forced to feel like you're odd
Out of place
Degenerate
Mad
Crazy
Ill
Unwell
Sick
Difficult
Disruptive
Obscene
Rebellious
Non conformists
Who need to be taught a swift lesson
And should be locked away
As outcasts
Until we learn the right way
And not to fly away on our own
But to follow
And keep in line

With those other ones
Who know not where they're heading
Or why
But submit to the will of strangers
Just because
That's the way they were told
The way it has always been
And they obey without thought
In fear of rocking the status quo
With question
Or query
Meanwhile
Glaring
And sneering
Frightful and frightened
Merely faces of the crowd
Jeering
Overbearing clowns
The collective mockery
Mocking you and I
The rebels they label misfits
Outside of our free minds
Perched on the wrong side of the fence
Where non conformity is a crime
An abomination to the blind
Following the blind
Punishable by ostracisation
We're the strange ones
Not permitted to fit in
For thinking outside the cage
Existing beyond

The accepted cultural norm
We're the ones in the wrong
And we've all been warned
If you choose to be different
You won't be the same
As everyone else
But if we chose to be the same
Then we wouldn't be being our self
We'd instead
Just be abiding by the rules
Siding with all the other fools
Blindness
Easily led
And our perspective skewed
But there's strength in dumbness
Psychological manipulation
Brings the sheep out in numbers
Lambs
Lead and lead and lead and lead
Until they now no longer need help
It's no trouble to cage a flock of birds
When taught to happily cage themselves.

INSTITUTE OF BARBERSHOP PSYCHOLOGY

It's funny about the course
Going to the college
The past year
Is the first time
That I've actually sat in a college
And learned anything
I left school at sixteen
I went off and was self-employed
I went straight to work from school
Barbering for six years
Cutting peoples hair
And doing hairdressing
Women's hair
Men's hair
All of that stuff
Working in various salons
Until I managed a salon as well
And that was me
Self-employed
Hands on
Creative
I've always been that way
Left school
And the one thing I could do
Was cut hair
And I went and got employment in that
But the reason
I went the whole hairdressing route
Hairdressing, such as colouring

Perming
Relaxing
Weave-ons
And all that kind of stuff
Is because I was naive
I was told, that's the way
That I would get into barbering
Which is what I actually wanted to do
So I went that route
Not knowing
That I could've just been a barber
I later realised I was advised
Based on the business interests
Of the company that I was working for
But by that point
I'd already learned all of it
I also learned about the world
And about people
About the way they think
When you're doing someone's hair
It's like you're their therapist
There's a bit of therapy going on
You get into their heads
And they're letting out all their thoughts
And their feelings
What they're going through
They will talk to you about it
Because you're in their head
I was sixteen, seventeen, eighteen
Nineteen and twenty
So I'm young

I'm learning about the world
These are grown people
Telling me their issues
And I'm hearing the person next to me
Who is doing someone else's hair
Hearing their client talking
About their issues
And their problems
Like real adult shit, you know
So I'm learning
When you're a kid like that
You're just soaking it all in
You're learning about the world and people
It was all very interesting to me
I guess a lot of it I didn't understand fully
But I was learning about how people think
And I understand it a hundred percent now
I mean, there's always more
But as an adult now
You understand
What a person was talking about
When they said their husband
Is not the man that she married
And he's doing this, and he's doing that
Or this other man
Thinks his wife is cheating
Or this other guy
Says he gets women because of his car
And as soon as he sleeps with them
He tells them to get out of his house
Or he'll call the police

That kind of stuff
That's some crazy stuff
When you think about it
There's a whole wide world out there
And I was learning about it
From a young age
Right from the source of the people
Who were living those lives
And happy to talk about it
Because you're in an environment
Where people come to vent
And they feel they can share
It's their little social place
The hairdressers
And the barbers
People talk and express themselves
And let things out
That's the environment I was in
At that young age
So I learned a lot about the world
And still learning
Even now
But it all definitely
Opened up the mind a lot.

IT'S TEARING ME APART

I'm discovering more of myself
I want to get more of myself out
Taking my fingernails
And digging into my stomach
So deeply
My nails are sharp
Piercing sharp
And I'm digging into my stomach
I'm tearing apart
I'm trying to rip out what's inside
And get to the very core of me
And see what's in there
And see how much I can pull out of me
Pulling out all of my insides
That's the metaphor
That's the analogy of it
That's what I'm trying to do
Trying to pull everything out
If I put it into a picture
Or a painting
That would be it
Or an image
A moving image
It would be me standing there
Pulling out all of my insides
Digging my nails deep
Into my own stomach
And just ripping out
Everything that's in there

Everything down to the bone
Down to the very innards
Ripping it all out
Just to discover what's in there
And get it all out
And show it
And share it
Like, look
That's what's inside of me
Look
All the blood coming out
All the gore
All the guts coming out
That's what's happening
That would be the picture of it
And I would hope
That people have some questions
Because then
If someone
Has some questions about it
Then there's more
Then I have to dig deeper
And find more
To answer
The questions that they have
Hopefully
Everything that I've shared
Would have answered any questions
But if there's any more questions
Then that's great
That means that I have to dig deeper

To answer those questions
Because I might not
Know the answer
I might have to dig deeper
To see what else is inside
To answer that question
If I've laid everything out
And there's still questions
Then I have to do more work
I have to do more digging
Because I may not even know
What the answer is
I may have to go do something
In myself
To answer that question
So, that would be good
More questions are better
I would hope that there is some
Because then
There's more work to be done
And that's great
That's heading towards completion
And if someone is inspired so much
That they have a question
About something they've seen
That they want to inquire further
That's great
We're doing something here
We're sharing
We're engaging together
We're connecting

We're learning
Let our curious minds go
Let's do it
Let's see what we're made of
Let's see why we're here.

KEEPING HER HUSBAND SATISFIED

My mum showed me a video
Of a woman
And she was talking about
How she's happy
For her husband to have other women
And they have a happy relationship
They've been together nineteen years
She chooses the women that he goes with
And the relationship is a happy one
She's not being forced to do it
Or anything like that
She finds that it's better for her
If she's supervising it
And feels it's okay
It's natural
And it's fine
It's just a different way of living
Or different to what we're used to
I think if you're married to someone
And then they want to have outside women
And you say that's fine
But only if you're choosing the women
And you're a woman yourself
I think that's another type of life
Another type of existence
You have to be able to deal with that
Or to even think that's okay
She's happy
For him to sleep with other women

She doesn't mind
But she chooses the women
She's the one who goes out
And selects the women for him
That's just another level
To what we know to be normal
Or what women would accept
Wives would accept
She enjoys watching
She often gets aroused
Watching him enjoying himself
With these women that she has selected
And she only selects the finest
According to her
She wants her man to have the best
So she goes out and gets quality
She makes sure these women
If he's going to have them
Are the cream of the crop
It's another world
There's a whole other world
Going on out here
To learn about
Though I would say
In all my years
That's rare
That's a rare thing
Compared to the ratio
Of where a woman
Is not going to accept
That her man is having other women

That's rare in comparison
To the ratio that would say
No, that's never going to happen
We're getting a divorce right now
Or whatever
The percentage is nowhere near
I don't think it's anything above 10%
Or 20% of married women
That would accept that
Or even be the woman
Who is going out
Selecting the women for him
For her husband to get down
And have fun with
In her presence
Never
She was saying
She'd rather be supervising it
Rather than him going out
And cheating
And she's happy for that
But that wasn't the only reason
She also says
She gets off on it
That she really enjoys is it.

LEARNING TO WIN

It's not something you can talk about
Unless you've experienced it
It's not something you can understand
Unless you've stood in that place
Lived it yourself
Sometimes
You're not even acknowledging the win
Because you're not used to it
It's having a win come your way
And writing it off as not for you
Even though it has your name on it
It's like no this is wrong
Someone must have made a mistake here
You don't really take on the win
As a winner should when they win
The celebration of it
Maybe you're expecting it
To be taken away at some point
It's a strange place to be
But sometimes
Some people
That's the only place they know
It's not really that strange to them
They're used to being there
It's definitely sad though
But when you realise it
And you've seen it from all angles
And you've acknowledged
What's happening with you

And how you think
And how things are happening around you
And you over stand the situation
It begins to feel a lot different
When you actually have acknowledged
That you deserve to win
That you deserve to be there
That this is a triumph
And you've earned it
When you get to that place
It's beautiful
It really is beautiful
I mean
Everyone deserves to win, right
Everyone who has persevered
Endured
Suffered
Done the work
Earned the place
They deserve to win.

LISTEN UP

I'm in the moment
I'm in the moment of listening
I'm actually listening
To what the person is saying to me
I'm actually listening
To what you're saying to me
And I find it funny
When people say to me
Are you listening

What it is
They wonder if I'm listening
Or if I'm even still on the phone
Because I'm so quiet
I'm paying attention
I'm listening
I'm processing
What's being said to me
I'm taking it in
I can actually respond
And tell you
Everything you just said

I find it funny
When people say are you there
Are you listening
Because I don't think
They're used to people
Listening to them

They're not used to people
Actually paying attention
To what they're saying

People don't listen
They listen with the intent to reply
Which means
They're always waiting to interrupt
Waiting for their next word
I'm a little fascinated by that
Because I listen
I'm paying attention
To what you're saying
That's why I'm quiet
I'm actually taking it in

I'm fascinated
Because people don't seem
To be used to that
They don't seem
To be used to people listening.

MOMENTS IN TIME

I know there are moments
In time
I know there are moments in time
That are happening
That may never repeat themselves
They may come in other forms
In other ways
But they're not going to come back
In the way they came at that moment
And in that energy that it was in
Or recorded in
The energy that may help somebody
Or I may need to know at that time
Or may need to refer to
In some way down the line
Or that just may be the moment
Sometimes you capture something
And it's that moment
You couldn't have got it a second time
If you try to do it a second time
It's not going to be the same
It's that moment
And thank God
I put on the camera sometimes
And record
Because I would miss so much magic
So much magic
It's going to change
Energy is always evolving

It's always changing
It's always going away
And coming back around
Like how the earth spins
It's going around
It comes back around again
And it meets the sun
And if you miss that
You've got to wait
Another hour
Another day
Another year
You've got to wait
Another hundred years
A thousand million years
For it to come back around again
It's like that
It's a moment
It'll come again
But it won't be the same
And it'll be another time
It won't be that time
And we're not around long enough
To miss those moments
That's how I feel.

NO EXTRACURRICULAR ACTIVITIES

When I get home
That's me for the evening
I'm just looking to head to my bed
And lay down and rest
And drift off into sleep early
I kind of cherish that these days
When I can get it
Or while I can get it
At this moment in time
Because very shortly
It'll be early mornings
All over again
Really early mornings
So I'm looking forward
To the rest time that I have now
So a nice early evening to bed
Is the best
Especially in this weather
It's nice to just get into your bed early
And just be cozy
And let the world carry on outside
As it does
And you don't have to be a part of it
That's a nice feeling
I don't get that often
Or at least
I don't take advantage of it often
So while I can
I will

That's one of the things
I'm looking forward to tonight
Just getting into my bed very shortly
And just being cozy and in bed
Just in bed
Not up
Not doing anything
Not out on the street
Not heading home late
None of that
Not traveling after hours
None of that stuff
Just in my bed
Just indoors
In bed
No extracurricular activities
Just me
And sleep
And bed
That's the plan
That is the plan.

ONE LIFE

Early start
No messing
Early as possible to bed
Hopefully if I can finish my work today
Then that means I can go to bed later
I won't need to go to bed so early
I only go to bed that early
Because I need to wake up
And be sharp
To do my homework before I leave
My homework make take a couple of hours
That's the only reason
I'm going to bed early
If I finish all my work today
At a decent hour
At least by ten o'clock
I can go to bed for eleven
Unwind for a bit
And just go to bed like I would normally
My normal routine
I haven't got that much left to do honestly
But because I'm thinking
About the presentation
I'm thinking about
How much I can memorise
And have the points in my head
That kind of thing
So I'll be taking my work to bed
As they say

But other than that
If I get the things
I need to do on the computer done
I can kind of relax a little bit
I'm kind of missing
All the free time I had
My weekends didn't matter
Even though I was out of my house
Before nine o'clock every morning
Even when
I didn't have to be anywhere necessarily
I just wanted to get to my second office
Third office
And do my work
That's just how I roll
This is it
One life, baby
One life.

ONE STONE A DAY

I've already impressed myself
Looking back
At what I've achieved
In the past year
Looking back at things I did
A year ago
And feeling impressed with myself
Proud of myself
Looking back a year ago to today
Things I did then
And from then till this point now
I'm feeling
That sense of accomplishment
And a sense of achievement
I'm actually doing it
It's nice
And that's just twelve months
So I imagine
How I would feel
In twenty-four months
Forty-eight months and so on
My friend always says
A stone a day raises a tower
And it's so true
A stone a day
And before you know it
You've got that sky high tower
That you've built yourself
Do I have off days

Feeling down
I don't have off days
If anything
I have off moments
And it's not long
Before I'm back in the right mode
In the positive mode
Back in the opposite to off day
I'm back on to on day very quickly
Just because of my wiring
And my conditioning
And things
That I've conditioned my mind with
That help me get back
Just understanding state changes
All the stuff I've learned from NLP
All of that just helps me
To not stay in that place
For very long at all
So I'll have off moments
But I'll never have off days
No way
I'll have off moments
Where I'll contemplate something
Or think negatively about something
Or feel off about something
Or down
But it won't really last long at all
I'm back in the swing in no time
It happens because I'm human
We're human

And it's likely to happen
I'm not He-Man
As much as I would like to be
Or as much as I think I am
I'm not
I'll be back in no time
One stone a day
Raises a tower.

ONE TYPE OF MOVIE I REALLY ENJOY

One of my favourite types of films to watch
Are films about the human spirit
Films about overcoming
Films about challenges and obstacles
And overcoming those challenges
And obstacles
Being triumphant
Going through some devastating situation
Or some setback of some kind
And coming through the other side
And how that is dealt with
Rising to the top
After being held down and held back
And a certain strength
Within the human spirit
Is required
To overcome those challenges
And those obstacles
I like films like that
They get me fired up
Because that's life really
I'll get fired up by those type of films
I could watch those types of films
All day long
One film like that is an animation film
Narrated by Matt Damon
It's called Spirit: Stallion of the Cimarron
A really great animation film about a horse
I love that film

Because it's all about that
They were trying to break his spirit
You're supposed to break a horse
To actually domesticate it
From being wild
That's what they were trying to do
With this horse
It was just the one horse
They couldn't break
Whatever they tried
They couldn't break it's spirit
It was all about that
I loved that film for that
Another film like that
Which has that kind of thing about it
Is Men of Honour
Starring Cuba Gooding Jr.
And Robert De Niro
It's a really good film
About that whole thing
Of being held back
Held down
Every time he tried
To advance forward
He was put down again
Tested
It's all about him
Being able to push himself
To the limits
To be the best
Because his dad always told him

Be the best
He instilled that in him from young
So films like that
Films about facing major challenges
And overcoming them
Another film like that
Is a film that Angelina Jolie directed
It's called Unbroken
That character, Louis Zamperini
Played by Jack O'Connell
Was just continually pushed
To the breaking point
But he always was so strong
And he carried on dealing with it
They were trying to break him
He was the one
That was singled out and bullied
By his superiors
It's just a really great film
It's very much about that overcoming
Rising above and not being broken
In the midst of people trying to break you
Break you down to nothing
Staying strong and rising above
Shawshank Redemption is like that too
With Tim Robbins and Morgan Freeman
I think that's a brilliant movie as well
For that same kind of overcoming
Another one is the movie Rocky
Starring Sylvester Stallone
A classic movie for that same thing

This small-town guy from nowhere
Who rises up and gets beat down
And comes back and is triumphant
The whole perseverance thing
That movie is a classic definition of that
I definitely come away with more
From films like that
Movies about overcoming
And pain, and struggle
And in the end, triumph.

SHE SOUNDS TOO GOOD TO BE TRUE

Apparently
I'm on the verge of having a woman
This is news to me
I asked, who is she then
If I could have a name
Or any clues or hints
Or to describe her perhaps
She's got a funny surname
I said, well if it goes well
We can change that
If she's anything
To write home about
He surname is not a problem
That will obviously get changed
If it goes well
If it's the fairy tale
So that's not an issue
What else
She looks like a little girl
I said, elaborate on that a little bit
You mean, she looks young for her age
I'm taking that as she looks young
For her age
Sometimes she looks like a boy
Okay, this is interesting
Keep going
You have to give me more
She's cute
Okay, that's a good start

A lot of potential
Is loving
Caring
Supportive and fun
Okay, these are all good things
Intelligent
That's definitely a winner
Worldly, good
Open-minded, good
Keep going
Cultured, that's good
Yeah, that's working
Great body, okay
Adding that to the list
Quirky, great
She doesn't sound familiar
But I'd be interested
In finding out more
This almost sounds
Too good to be true
I shall look forward
To hearing more about her.

SHE'D HAVE TEN HUNDRED ORGASMS

In the dark
Black or white wouldn't matter
Because you can't see the person
But they're doing the exact same thing
That you couldn't hold back from
It's the same feeling and sensation
The dark
Takes away a lot of those senses
It takes away race
And it takes away gender
A lot of those things
That create fear
Inhibitions
White
Black
Male
Female
Imagine a woman
Who is a lesbian
A proper feminist
Hardcore lesbian
Doesn't like men
Can't stand men
Hates men
But yet
She's in a dark room
She doesn't know its a man
Who is going down on her
This man knows exactly what to do

What spots to hit
He's even had information
From her ex girlfriend
Who knows her body well
And what she would like
How she likes it
He's going to do
Exactly what he's been told
And how she would enjoy it
She would not know
She'd have ten hundred orgasms
And not know it's a man down there
Giving them to her
That just real
It eliminates a lot of stuff
When those senses are taken away
When we're not dealing with race
When we're not dealing with our fears
And opinions
Of white and black
Our opinions of male and female
When all of that is taken away
And you're just dealing with the senses
And touch and sensation
It's all open then
The floodgates are open
Excuse the pun.

SOMETIMES SEX DISGUSTS ME

I'll be honest with you
I'm a man
I like to see a bit of nudity, yes
In a very man way
But I think
I'm going away from that
This is the honest truth
I go in and out of phases
Where I like to see nudity
And then it actually disgusts me
I like the idea of sex
And then the thought
Actually disgusts me
I go through phases
Where I'm one or the other
That's the honest truth
There's times
Where it's the last thing I want to see
And I want to get myself as far away
From the idea of it
Or putting myself in situations
Where it can arise
And then there's other times
I want to immerse myself in it
Excuse the pun
That's the honest truth
There's times I go through phases
Right now
My mind is quite heavily
Into sex transmutation
It's something I go in and out of

Reading about
Thinking about
Considering the whole celibacy thing
And abstinence
I just go through phases with it all
There are times
I think about sex with a woman
And the idea just turns me off
I just think ugh
I really do
I swear to god
And there's other times I want some
And then other times
I'm just like no
That's ugh
No thanks
I really do
I really go through these phases
Of this whole being a man thing
I just want sex
And then
I go through this thing of ugh
No, it disgusts me
Even the thought of it
It's dirty
I really do
I swear to god
That's the truth.

STYLISH DESIGNER COAT

I'm at a vintage fair right now
My friend is trying on a very expensive coat
It's a very nice coat
It's the only one of its kind
The guy makes these coats
And these outfits himself
It's a really nice coat
It's definitely worth
The five hundred pounds
It's a one-off
It looks great
I definitely would say to him buy it
If he likes it
He should get it
Apparently
This coat
Can be worn seven different ways
Well, for that price
For a long black coat
You should be able to
Wear it in more than one way for sure
But it definitely looks great
It definitely looks expensive
And it's the only one like it he's made
So you know
It's one of those one-off rare items
You would probably be glad you bought
Or would definitely look unique in
If you were wearing it out somewhere

You turn up to a place
And people can see that it's unique
An expensive looking item you're wearing
That kind of thing
Is sometimes worth the money
Worth spending the extra cash
If you have it to spend, of course
Me, I'm just here as a spectator
I'm not buying a five hundred pound coat
Or looking to buy one at the moment
I've got better things to do with my money
Than wear it
But you know how it is
I say why not
It looks good on him
He should splash his cash
He's talking
With the designer who made it
I think he may indeed buy it
We'll see what unfolds
In the story of the stylish designer coat.

TATTOO EXPRESSION

Getting a tattoo is majorly addictive
I got my first one as a teenager
It's very addictive
I don't think I'd get any more
That was my first one
And I carried on getting tattoos
Until I was twenty-two
I was in the zone of getting tattoos
It's basically addictive
I liked it
I liked the ink
I liked the inner work
Of mentally dealing
With my threshold for pain
I still think there's something to that as well
I got my last tattoo when I was twenty-two
Twenty years later
I don't think I'll get any more now
But it's very addictive
And you have to be very careful
Luckily for me
I tattooed things
That I would always be happy about getting
Things that were meaningful to me
It's not like I had some drunken night
Away on holiday somewhere
And said, Hey let's get a tattoo
And then woke up the next morning
Like, what the fuck did I do

I was always very in tune as a youngster
And was always aware of what I was doing
I wouldn't have gone
And just gotten any old tattoo
If I was going to do something
It would have to have meaning to it
For a tattoo
It would have to be something
That was going to mean something
Or that I'd always want to see
Or be reminded of
When I looked at myself
I was at least that smart
So I got things that were meaningful
I was thinking the other day
I'm glad I've got these on me
Because it's stuff that I would want
To be reminded of if I'm ever off-centre
It's stuff that I would look at
And it would bring it back to the source
Of what it's about for me
Myself and life
And the purpose of things
I was lucky in that sense
I don't know if luck is the word
But I was definitely blessed in that sense
To get stuff that I wouldn't regret
Later on down the line
I don't think I'd get any more though
I think I would but I haven't felt the urge
To go and get anything yet

I just haven't got into that zone yet
But I do think I possibly would
If there was something I liked
And I thought to myself
I have to have this on my body
I want this to be with me forever
I just haven't got into that zone yet
I haven't thought about it enough
I'm quite happy with what I have
I guess maybe that time hasn't come
Maybe it's passed, maybe it was a phase
I'm not thinking tattoo
Or what's my next tattoo
I'm not thinking like that
I put it down in written form now
To speak out
Or written poetry
Or recording the audio of my words
As opposed to recording on my skin
I would've run out of space by now
I'd look like those completely inked guys
That just have no natural skin colour left
It's just all tattoo ink all over their bodies
I'd be overwriting by now
I feel like it was a form of expression
Before I found more concrete ways
To express myself
That's one of the reasons why
I don't think I would get any more
Because I've found other ways
To express myself

And share my thoughts and ideas
And things that are meaningful to me
Other than putting it on my skin
I've found other solid ways
For me to express myself
And to make a mark
Those are the reasons why
I wouldn't necessarily get
Or feel the need to get another tattoo
And that may change
But right now I don't feel like I need it
I have other ways to express myself
And share my thoughts
And record those thoughts and ideas
To save them from getting away from me
Essentially, inking is there for others to see
People could argue that it's there
For themselves to see and read
I've got other ways to share my thoughts
And how I feel about the world right now
So I no longer need to go put it on my body
I've got a bigger audience now
To reach with all my concepts
Other than just when I take my shirt off
Or at home in the mirror
Or with someone I'm naked with
I've got much bigger broader ways
To express myself now in that way
When I want to create forms of permanence
So it's probably one of the reasons
I won't be inked out.

THE IMPORTANCE OF FOREPLAY & ORAL SEX

How important is foreplay to you
Foreplay
Oral sex
It's important
It's majorly important
I think it's the thing
That gets the wheels turning
It's foreplay
It's the thing you do before you play
I think anyone who doesn't see fit
To engage in foreplay
Is not fit to play at all
That's just my view
I mean it gets the juices flowing
It just does
It's just good
There's nothing wrong with it
It's this taboo thing
I don't know why
It's okay to play before you play
People are happy to receive
But not to give
And there is a problem with that
It's a two-player game
You must get involved
It's the warmup
It's the stretch
It's the early rehearsal for the big game
You need to loosen up

It's just good
I'm an advocate for foreplay
I'm an advocate for oral sex
I have no problem with it at all
I recommend it
I've never had a problem with it
I'm not against it
I just don't see what the big fuss is about
And why it's such a taboo thing
It's part of the lovemaking experience
It's part of intimacy
It just is
It's not evil
It's not all these negative things
That I hear people talking about
When they're describing it
Or expressing their views about it
Not for me anyway
It's not a bad thing
It's a great thing
It's something to be celebrated
It's a thing that you can share with a person
And you can provide pleasure
And give satisfaction to someone
It's a beautiful thing
It should be loved
Cherished and appreciated
And enjoyed
Just as much as sex itself
It's part of sex
It's the I appreciate you

I want to give you pleasure
I want to make you feel good
I care about how you feel
I want to give you satisfaction
I want to relax you
I want to share that with you
So much can be said about it
I'm sure you have your own views
In regards to the whole topic
Giving and receiving
I know there's people out there
That prefer receiving to giving
If I'm honest with you
I find that it is a thing
That I get pleasure
Out of giving the pleasure
I receive pleasure from that
As much as I enjoy receiving
I enjoy giving as well
I just get high off of the giving
As well as the receiving pleasure of oral sex
And of foreplay in general
It's the foreplay that your parents played
Before you got here
And their fore-parents before them
And so on and so forth
So let's get to foreplaying
Before we don't get to play at all
I don't have to be a woman
To know what women like
I just have to have been practicing

I just have to have been a practitioner
A listener
It requires listening
Listening to a woman's body
Listening to a man's body
If you're a woman
Or whatever you are
Whatever you do
And however you get down
It's about listening
To the other person's body
You have to be able to listen to reactions
How they're feeling
How you're making them feel
How they're responding
All of that stuff
I have absolutely no problem
If I am into somebody
I am going downtown
I am going down south
I am in there like swimwear
Trust me
It's not a problem to me
I don't know why it's such an issue
Especially the guy thing
I hear so many women
Talking about guys
Not being into it
All of these reasons
And excuses
I see memes online

And things across the internet
And I thought I'd get involved
In the conversation somewhat
Or at least put in my ten pence
My two pence
My one pence
My thoughts
My feelings
My standpoint on it as a guy
I think there needs to be some input there
More in-depth than your odd comment
And reaction
To what a female may have posted online
I wanted to add something
To the conversation
So here I am
On the record
Saying how I feel about the subject
I would say all my many years
As a practitioner
In the area, so to speak
Qualifies me as an authority
To speak on the subject
I have written poetry about this subject
I have recorded poetry about this subject
I have performed poetry
In front of live audiences
About this subject
You may notice
I am passionate about this subject

We're just not talking
About the things that matter
The important things
That we should all be discussing
We're just not doing it
The things like this
That really matter
Now with all of that said
And lest we forget
Let's keep it clean
No one wants a cardiac arrest
From uncleanness or uncleanliness
So let's keep it tip-top
Top of the line clean and fresh
It's important
Very important
Extremely important
It's a must do
Before we even consider it
Let's keep that in mind
Keep it clean, keep it clean
Everyone has a view about it
Everyone has a thought about it
Even if they don't express it
Their own personal feelings about it
Or stuff they've expressed
With only friends
Or whoever
Or their partner
Or maybe haven't expressed it
With their partner

Maybe they should, maybe they should
I just wanted to share my two pence
My own thoughts about it
To you
What are your thoughts on oral sex
And foreplay
And how important is it to you
In regards to intimacy
What do you think
Are you for it
Or against.

THE NECESSITY OF LETTING THINGS OUT

All of this has been my outlet
From drawing to writing to video
Whatever it might be
Creative
Artistic
It has all been my expressive outlet
My catharsis
It's like constipation
If you were eating, eating, eating
And you never went to the toilet
That wouldn't be good for you
It's like that
It's why I said, it's killing us
Because we have all these emotions
And feelings and experiences
Built up inside of us
But we're not expressing them
We're not sharing how we really feel
We're not talking about things
We're not exhaling and letting it out
And that's what's killing us
People don't realise
That's a lot of the reason
For like things like mental health
And all these things that happen
And how people snap
And just go and do things
That put them in serious trouble
In a moment of madness

Because there was pent up stuff
And then something came
That made them just snap
And that's when it all came out
Everything
It was nothing to do
With the situation that was at hand
But everything else came with it
Like a river
Like a flood when the dam breaks
And all the water flows out
Comes crashing out
Finally
Bringing everything with it
With a seemingly vengeful fury
An aggressive outburst
It's the pressure.

THE NEXT BEST THING

Imagine
What's the next best thing
You lost that stuff
All that stuff you recorded
And all of that stuff you documented
But what's the next best thing
Continue I would say
Just keep going
Carry on from where you left off
Just keep going
Imagine in ten years from now
Even if you were just starting now
To just do it
Like you'd never done anything before
Forget all the stuff you lost from then
That's nearly ten years
Nearly ten years of stuff you don't have
But I'm thinking, what's the next best thing
Okay, you've lost ten years of stuff
But what's the next best thing
When another ten years happens
What would have been the next best thing
To continue where you left off
Where it went wrong
Rather than dwelling
On the last ten years
For the next ten years
And then having twenty years of nothing
That's what it would be

That wouldn't be a nice place to be
In my mind
When you get to old age
And you look back
You realise
Every moment was a special moment
But by that point it's too late
When you're too old
To do anything about it
Every moment
Is a special moment really
When you think about it
You need to put it out there
It's your story
You get to tell it
How'd it go down
Who were you
Why are you here
Why were you here
In whatever way you choose
I hope everybody documents their life
Documents aspects of their life
Or parts of their day
In some way
Evidence
That they were even fucking here
On the planet.

THE RIGHT WAY

There are no directions
Most of the time
You're standing at a crossroad
And there are multiple ways to turn
You never really know
Whether you're on the right road
Whether you're going the right way
You just have to keep putting
One foot in front of the other
And keep it moving
Trusting that there will be light
At the end of the road
There will be a sign
That tells you
You've made the right choice
And you're going the right way
In some ways, there is no right way
You just have to trust
Based on the decisions you're making
And the direction you're going in
That it will lead you
To the place you ultimately want to be in
And keep it moving
There's never really someone
At that crossroad
To say, yep, this way
You're going the right way
There never really is that
And when there is

You're still never sure
Only you can know for yourself
Whether your direction
Is the right direction for you
Based on where you want to be
And where you feel comfortable
But one thing is for sure
You know when it's right
You feel it
And it feels good
You just have to keep going
For as long as it feels right
You never really know
It's like walking in darkness
And trusting
Each step forward
Is going to lead you somewhere
That is not detrimental to your journey
To yourself
There is a lot of trust involved
There is a lot of trusting yourself
That you're making the right decisions
And you're going in the right direction
That gut feeling
Following your instinct
You never really know
But you do know
When it feels right
And that's as good as knowing
That you're doing the right thing
And going the right way.

THE SECRET WAR

After a while
The voices quieten
After a time
Some seemingly stop completely
Either that or you've come to learn
How to tune them out
Until the only one you hear now
Is your own
These days I couldn't care less
Who's talking bad about me
Wish them my best
They'll have to chat without me
There's more pressing things
In my world
I'm more invested in
Than men gossiping like girls
With women I'm no longer interested in
I've been onto wiser and better things
There comes a time to grow up
And leave behind the lesser things
Small minds stay small time
And wonder why they never win
All in all, I'm over everything
Like a bird in the sky
Learning to fly again
I've tried and tried
I've been tried and tried
I've been tired
But I've tried again

You come to learn in time
Your only opponent
Is your mind
Time to own it
And make amends
Time to grow
Where you're going shows
It needs no explanation
Time to go
Eyes forward
Focused on the journey
And the destination
Obstacles come
And shall be overcome
That has to be in how you think
An ocean of deep thoughts
Can overwhelm
And throw you off course
And that's how you sink
But a drowning man
Is a desperate man
Never underestimate the tormented
When his back is against the wall
And it's his life or death
A man can get extremely inventive
Summoning things from within
From places he's never been
Bringing forth power and an inner light
That other minds have never seen
Minds that believe in no god
In any faith, form or fraction

And thus believe
There's no consequence to their actions
They rape
They lie
They plunder
They pillage
Then wonder why
The kids set fire to the village
Young ones
Burnt hands
Angry faces covered in soot, blood and tears
Their finest work is far from done
And thus, should be feared
Our soul
Our spirit
Our energy
Never die
There's memory in our DNA
That just won't go away
It keeps transferring
From form to form
Beyond time and space
Once we are, we are
And once it is, it is
And cannot
Be erased.

THE WORKINGS

It's so interesting
How processes are transferable
There are similar processes
And preparations
A painter will go through
That are very similar
To the way a dancer may prepare
Which is really interesting
Or a musician
Or a sculptor
Or a writer
A singer
There's processes
That are transferable
Because there's always this place
You have to go to within
And without
And I just find it so interesting
And I love process
I'm just fascinated by it
I just love the way it all works
The inner workings
And the outer workings
Of creativity
Is a beautiful subject to me
And a beautiful undertaking
If you're an artist
I think it's just wonderful
I love it

And I think that's why
I'll always be creative
And always have been
For some people
Creativity is like their oxygen
It's close to breathing
It's necessary.

TRACES OF YOU

I can't see your face
But I can feel you
I see traces of you
Walking ahead of me
In long flowing red satin
There's pleasure in your stride
Your glances back towards me
As you move from place to place
And I willingly follow you
The traces of you
You're aware of me
Which tells me everything you do
In these moments
Is with me in mind
That makes me smile
Along with every thought of you
Traces of you
Inside free-flowing white linen
Your glide is soft and graceful
Your slow stride and step are seducing
Mesmerising like music
Your movements, smooth
Like slow motion in the air
Your energy overpowers
Yet like your touch, is soft
Like your skin
In traces of you
Your eyes glisten and shine
Calling me in

Your smile is bright and warming
Bringing in a peaceful ray of light
On days like this
I want to stay forever
In the presence of floating beauty
Enveloped and enraptured
In the traces of you.

WE HAVE KIDS, PLEASE DON'T SHOOT

Yesterday
A girl posted on her blog
That she would never ever date or be with
Any person who already has children
Immediately I felt compelled to write to her
So I did
I wrote
You are definitely not the only one
Who feels that way
There are many others
Who would say the same for themselves too
But as time passes
And with age
And with more relationship
And life experience
Our feelings about how important that is
More often than not
Change
Those same little children
Will have all grown up
Become independent
And will have left home
And had kids of their own
Those people who felt that way
If they're still single
Which very often they remain
Depending on how strongly
They feel this way
And for how long

Tend to change their perspective
The older people get
It becomes more and more likely
That any prospective partners they meet
Will have already had children
Unless he or she
Chooses to seek
Outside the school gates
A much younger partner than themselves
They will otherwise
Have matured
Into just wanting simply to find someone
Who loves and cares about them
Whom they can be happy with
And with whom they can spend and enjoy
What is left of their life
The fact that someone already has children
Becomes somewhat expected
And far less of an issue by such time
Some realise
And grow into this truth earlier
Some later
Again, this is dependant
On how passionate they are
About not wanting to be with someone
Who already has kids
Every time you shoot down a person
Just because they have children
You're possibly shooting down
What could potentially
Be the love of your life

And after pulling the trigger
You'd never know
It is sad to realise all of this too late
When we've become less attractive
Less youthful
And much older
And eventually dependant
Like those same children ourselves
And end up just living and dying
Without anyone
All alone
With nothing but sorrow
And the cold company
Of our own painful regrets
I thought very much like her
When I was younger
But just like any of my friends
I no longer feel that way today
Time teaches us all in hindsight
I felt moved
To just offer her some food for thought
And a different perspective to consider
Something I wish I'd been offered myself
Much earlier in life.

WHAT I KNOW

If it's something that I know
That I'm talking about
Then yeah I can go
I'm not going to talk
About stuff I don't know about
If I'm in a place there
Where I'm out of my depth
I'm not going to even play in that arena
I'm just going to say I don't know
I can't speak on that
I don't really know enough about it
But if it's something I know
I've lived
I've experienced
Then yeah I'm going to talk for the world
Because I know what I'm talking about
And that's the place I like to be at
I like to know what I'm talking about
If someone asked me a question
About the subject
And I have a knowledge on it
Or have experience in it
Or both
I can go
I can talk
Because I know what I'm talking about
The worst thing for me to do
Is to be talking about something
I don't know what the fuck

I'm talking about
I'm just not into that
If I don't know
I say I don't know
And I have no problem not knowing
Because I don't know everything
I'm going to say I don't know
And I'm going to probably talk about
Something that I know
Because I think
That's what people should do
Talk about the shit you know
I've got a lot more of a song to sing
If I'm singing about something I know
And I know the words and everything
And the melodies and where the bridge is
And the chorus is
And all the rest of it
I'm going to sing that song
At the top of my voice
I'm not going to be as if I don't know
I don't know the words
So I don't know what I'm talking about
I don't know what I'm singing about
Forget that
There's no joy in that
I rejoice
At talking
About the stuff I know about.

WHAT YOU DON'T KNOW WILL THRILL YOU

If it's pitch-black
And someone's performing
Cunnilingus or fellatio on you
And you can't see
Who they are
What they are
I don't think
You're going to feel any different
Once they're hitting the right spots
You're going to have the same experience
You're going to have
The same happy ending
Aren't you
They're using the same tools as anyone else
I don't care what anyone says
That's a fact
It's not going to be any different
Once the person is doing the same things
That work for you
No matter what gender they are
And you can't see them
You're going to have the same experience
At the end of it
That's just plain
You're not in control of it
You can't see
All you know is
You're getting the same sensations

And experiencing the same thrills
That you would normally experience
When the best thing is happening to you
When your favourite thing
Is happening to you
In the way that you like it
You're going to have the same end result
No matter what
Because you can't see
You don't know who they are
It's common sense
It's plain
There's no other way to say it
You wouldn't know
So you're going lay back
And think of happy endings
It's not going to matter
Because you don't know who's doing it
If you're there in the experience
To have the experience
And you're not allowed to know who it is
And you've accepted
That you're not going know who it is
Ever
And they're hitting the spots
That you like
You're going to be happy
You're not going to feel any different
You're not going to know any different
That's an open mind for you
Would I try it

I think I would
For the simple fact
That I wouldn't know
And I can't see
It'd be interesting
That's real
I'll tell it as it is.

WHEN I'M GONE

When you go
You're remembered for a few days
People speak well of you
A few may shed a tear
Some share an endearing story or two
Maybe you'll get two weeks
If you were a popular soul
After that
Only those closest
Or who were drawn to you
Recall you on your birthdays
Then after a time
They too begin to forget
Your face
Your voice
Your words
Your energy
Eventually
We all fade from memory
And time
When I'm gone
Gather with your friends and family
And any whom share affinity for me
Set a flame to burn and release a bird
As someone reads aloud these words
Light some soft scented candles around
Lay bright and pretty flowers down
And some thoughtful words of your own
I'll be all around you and within you

Wherever you are, will be my home
When I'm gone
Choose my words carefully
Post them up on the walls
In places where men and women learn
And wherever children play
Not forgetting, where adults have fun time
And where the children study
May they all read questioningly
And thoughtfully
May they hear within, ponder and reflect
As you do now
When I'm gone
Know that I too also knew
That I could have done
And should have done much better in life
In success and achievement
In love
As a father
As a son
As a brother
As a human being
Rest assured and find some comfort
In the fact that this truth
Will never be as painful
And disappointing to bear
For you, as it always was for me
In all the places I failed you
And myself
When I'm gone
I like to think of all the women

With whom I've been closely intimate
And shared my sacred energy with
Gathered around together
With children and grandchildren
Recounting stories
And significant moments
Memories of our times together
I like to think each will say
Their encounters with me
Were uniquely special
Like no other they'd ever experienced
At any time with anyone else
And that I wasn't at fault
For not loving them
More than I loved myself
When I'm gone
I hope that my words appeal to you
Teach you and heal you
In ways I'd always aimed for in life
But knew might only be achieved
In absence
Often our words are only celebrated
Long after we've vacated
I'd made my peace with that long ago
The living ones won't proclaim to know it
Though history will plainly show it
That mainly the best poet is the dead poet
When I'm gone
Know that all wrongs towards me
Are forgiven
All transgressions forgotten

That I've taken none of them with me
They were far too heavy for the journey
And unnecessary to bear
Picture me complete
At the dawn of a new sunset
Strolling the shore
Of my souls favourite place
Smiling to the gentle crashing of waves
As the rough tide calmly rolls away
And welcomes in
A warm close of day.

WHO SHOULD PAY ON A DATE?

I believe
That when two people
Are going on a date
In regards to who should pay
I think in this modern age
In this modern era
That the person who pays
Should be the person
Whose idea it was to go on a date
Whoever asks the person out
On the date
I think
In this equal opportunity age
And era
And time of our lives
And going forward
I think that whoever approached
Regarding the idea of a date
And whatever form
That date takes shape
I think that person
Should be prepared to pay
Because a part of me
As old fashioned as I am
Thinks that it is absolutely crazy
That a woman
Is going to ask a man on a date
Or suggest a date
Or propose a date

And then expect him
To pay the bill for the date
I think that is absolutely ludicrous
As old-fashioned as I am
I think
There's some level
Of craziness to that
Unfairness
Inequality
Where's the equal opportunity in that
That a woman
Should ask a man on a date
He says yes
I will go on a date with you
And she expects
Him to pay for the date
To foot the bill
Ludicrous
I think it should be
If he so sees fit to pay
If he feels he wants to do that
To extend that courtesy
I feel that should be up to him
And he should not be held
In any way
Obliged to do that
I feel if he wants to
It is up to him
It shouldn't at all be expected
And he should not be considered bad
Or whatever

One might want to label him
For not wanting to pay
Or not paying
Because he was asked on a date
I feel
He should not have to suffer that
Whoever suggests the date
Should at the very least
Suggest splitting the expense
Right down the middle
In the absence of that suggestion
I feel it should be the person
That asked the other to go on the date
Or that suggested the date
That should also suggest
And expect for themselves
To be the person
Who pays for the date.

WHY I MIGHT NEVER GET MARRIED

I don't believe in toxic relationships
The whole staying married thing
Because of these vows and stuff
I think that was of a time
I think that whole thing is decaying now
It's like a decaying building
It's like a building that's falling apart
The structure is falling apart
And people are running out
Running out of an abandoned building
That's about to fall down
It's like that
It's like the whole structure of marriage
The whole construct is not what it was
Maybe it was just never going to work
It was never going to stay standing
I don't see myself ever getting married
Were we ever supposed to get married
I don't mean marriage between two souls
I mean marriage in a church
A building
Or designated place somewhere
On a particular day
And put on a ring
And declare it a marriage by law
I don't think it works
I think it's decaying
I think people are just following a construct
I think it's the thing to do

It's what your parents did
Or didn't do but should have
According to what is considered decent
Or is the acceptable norm
To get married to somebody
And have children
And settle down
Society has it
That if you're not doing it
You're not following convention
You're not following this construct
That's been there for however long
I don't know
I just don't think it works today
People make it work
They stay together
Because they've made
Those vows to do that
And they honour them
And they stay together
Even when it's not working
Even when it's just falling apart
At the seams
And it's all crashing down
Bit by bit
There may come a time
Where marriage
Is not a thing anymore
Where people
Just don't bother anymore
They don't get married

Because for them
It's just all changed
The true meaning of marriage
They've changed
They're just evolved
Into some other thing
Where people
Don't even respect marriage anymore
To actually even do it
The idea of going and getting married
Just fizzles out
No one really does it anymore
Like phone cards
Or rotary phones
Or old coins or something
That have become kind of obsolete
It's just the thing to do
That's why people get married
After being together fourteen years
I don't know
What do I know
But I just think
It's definitely a construct
That is collapsing
And everyone's running out of it
That's what I currently see it as
People are not valuing marriage
The way they did before
Let's get out of here
Let's not even go in here
In the first place

It's just this whole thing
That's falling down
And people are just getting out
As quick as they can
Soon it's going to be no more
It's going to just crumble to nothing
People don't value marriage
People don't seem to value
These vows they're taking
Don't get me wrong
There's plenty of people that do
But there's so many that don't
They're getting married
And they're looking
For someone to sleep with
And have a relationship with
While they're in a relationship
With in their partner or spouse
They don't respect the vows
I haven't seen enough
Of a positive image of marriage
To say, I want to do that one day
As I've got older and seen more
And my eyes are more open
And I've seen relationships
And how they work
And all of the things
That go on behind the scenes
And behind people's back
I just don't subscribe to that
The idea that I will be married

I don't see it for myself
I mean, I'm sure
There's plenty of couples
That are together
And have stayed together
In marriage, in holy matrimony
And are completely happy
But I just don't know them
I just haven't been exposed to it
To the degree where I can say
Yeah, I want to be like that one day
I just haven't had enough
Positive examples in my life
Marriage is a myth to me
I think the marriage starts
Way before any decisions
To get engaged
And announce it to family
And buy a dress
And get a ring
To go to a church
Say I do
All that stuff
I think the marriage
Should have long started
Way before all of that
That's how I feel.

YOU'RE ON YOUR OWN

Unfortunately
Life doesn't come with a warning sign
There's no instruction manual
Code of conduct
Or reference guide
Handed to you on arrival
No formal introduction
No rule book
Or list of dos and don'ts
Posted up in the waiting area
No toolbox talk
Or written statement of particulars
Or safety awareness program
Issued to you on your way in
There's no fully experienced
Member of the team
To meet and greet you at the start
Who will be with you
Every step of the way
To take you through
All stages of the program
And to answer
All of your questions and concerns
Their only concern
Is that you don't ask them
Too many questions
Knowing
That they don't have all the answers either
There's no one available

Who is fully qualified enough
To take out and remove
All of life's guess work
You'll be figuring it all out as you go along
There's no one on hand
Who knows every one of the blind spots
And possible pitfalls
That you may encounter
Throughout the course
Of your training period
No one to hold your hand
Who knows their way
Confidently
Through all of the dark spaces
You will inevitably find yourself in
There will be no light
At the end of the tunnel
Until of course
You know where you're going
There's no dummy run
No panic button
No emergency break glass
No search and rescue
No hazard lights
No seat belts
No breaks
No oxygen masks
No air bag
No fire drill
No crash test
No get-out clause

No do-over
No rerun
No rehearsal
No saving grace
And no knight in shining armour
You soon come to find
That all and any emergency helplines
Are busy
With no one really having the time to listen
You're free however
To talk to yourself, of course
But that's only if time permits
Self awareness
Self reflection
Self discovery
Self preservation
You come to discover
That there's actually no one dedicated team
Manning the office
That you're on your own
And no-one really knows who's in charge
And that inevitably
You too will end up
Eventually having to work from home
And off of your own initiative, alone
In other words
You'll have to learn
To master your own mind
Those who don't quickly find a way
To become their own boss
Eventually get lost

And there will be no pity party
Sent to find you
And rescue you from the inevitability
Of your internal wars
These are unique battles
Ones you'll be forced to fight alone
And by yourself
Until the day you die
Or are reborn
There will be no peace offering
That's something you'll have to find
On your own
And give to yourself
There will be no relent
And no surrender
From all that life wants to give to you
Or to take away
And no special concessions
Or blessings
That in some way you didn't earn
There's only but one way
To hand in your notice
To quit
Or to leave
This is the sworn contract
Between you and life
Already signed and sealed
By your ultimate and involuntary arrival
And therefore
Can never be broken.

ABOUT THE AUTHOR

Phoenix James is an award winning Writer, Poet, Author and Spoken Word Recording Artist. He began performing his poetic words live on stages across the UK in 1998. His debut spoken word poetry album, *The A.R.T.I.S.T,* was released in 2000. His first limited edition printed collection of poetry, *To Whom It May Concern,* was published in 2003. He has toured and performed his poetry internationally since 2004. He has appeared in films, on television and radio shows, and collaborated with other artists, singer-songwriters, actors, musicians, filmmakers and producers. In 2013, he wrote, directed and produced the feature length mock documentary film, *Love Freely but Pay for Sex.* Phoenix James is the author of several poetry collections and has recorded and released several spoken word poetry albums including *Phenzwaan Now & Forever, A Patchwork Remedy for A Broken Melody, FREE, Haven for the Tormented, With All That Said, Light Beams from the Void,* and over sixty spoken word poetry singles. All are available online now and streaming everywhere worldwide.

If you enjoyed reading this book, please leave a review or comment online. The author reads every review and they help new readers discover his work.

PHOENIX JAMES

Photo by Phoenix James

Phoenix James lives in London, England.

Connect with Phoenix James on his online social media platforms via www.linktr.ee/Phoenix_James and say you've read this book. To contact or learn more about Phoenix James and his creative journey or to receive updates via his Newsletter Mailing List, visit his official website at www.PhoenixJamesOfficial.com

Phoenix James Official

www.ingramcontent.com/pod-product-compliance
Lightning Source LLC
Chambersburg PA
CBHW021238090426
42740CB00006B/593